Eyewitness
ROCKS &
MINERALS
Expert Files

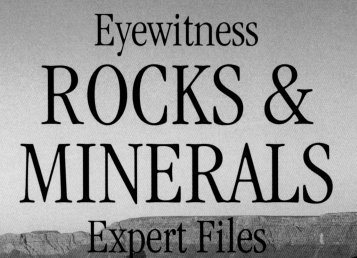

Eyewitness
ROCKS &
MINERALS
Expert Files

DK Publishing Inc

LONDON, NEW YORK,
MELBOURNE, MUNICH, AND DELHI

Consultant Douglas Palmer
Senior Editor Jayne Miller
Project Editors Sarah Davis, Jaqueline Fortey
Senior Art Editors Joanne Little, David Ball
Art Editors Owen Peyton Jones, Peter Radcliffe,
Susan St.Louis, Gemma Thompson
Paper Engineer Ruth Wickings
Managing Editor Camilla Hallinan
Art Director Martin Wilson
Publishing Manager Sunita Gahir
Category Publisher Andrea Pinnington
Picture Research Fran Vargo
DK Picture Library Rose Horridge, Claire Bowers
Production Controller Angela Graef
DTP Designers Ronaldo Julien, Andy Hilliard
Jacket Designer Polly Appleton
Jacket Copywriter John Searcy

First published in the United States in 2007
by DK Publishing Limited,
375 Hudson Street, New York, New York 10014

07 08 09 10 11 10 9 8 7 6 5 4 3 2 1
ED508 – 07/07

A catalog record for this book is available
from the Library of Congress.

ISBN: 978–0–7566–3132–1

Color reproduction by Colourscan, Singapore
Printed and bound by Toppan Printing Co.
(Shenzhen) Ltd, China

Discover more at
www.dk.com

Contents

1

MEET THE EXPERTS

Rock and mineral experts investigate Earth. For some, this can mean getting up close to volcanoes. Expert Marie Edmonds explains what it's like to feel the heat.

EXPERT
Volcanologist
PROFILE

NAME: **MARIE EDMONDS**

LOCATION: **MONTSERRAT**

HOME COUNTRY: **UK**

Right out of college in 2001, Marie Edmonds' first job as a qualified volcanologist took her to the observatory of the Soufrière Hills Volcano in Montserrat, an island in the Caribbean. The Montserrat Volcano Observatory was set up in 1995 after a massive eruption devastated the island. In fact, the volcano has been erupting steadily ever since. The highest levels of activity occurred in 1997, killing 26 people. The observatory staff monitors volcanic activity above and below the ground and warns locals living in its shadow of the level of danger, evacuating them if necessary. Marie lived on the island, monitoring and researching the volcano, for three years.

BEFORE THE ERUPTIONS
Montserrat was once a thriving island whose local population survived by farming and tourism. Much of the lush green land now lies buried under ash from the eruption of 1995 and later outpourings.

Deathly Dust

HUGE CLOUDS OF ASH DARKEN THE SKY ABOVE THE ISLAND OF MONTSERRAT. WHEN THE SOUFRIERE HILLS VOLCANO EXPLODED IN 1995, IT WAS THE FIRST TIME IT HAD ERUPTED FOR 350 YEARS. THIS ERUPTION HAS BEEN CONTINUING EVER SINCE.

Gulf of Mexico

Cuba

Caribbean Sea

Montserrat

PACIFIC OCEAN

South America

MONTSERRAT ON THE MAP
Montserrat belongs to a group of islands known as the Leeward Islands in the Caribbean.

ERUPTING FORCE
Soufrière Hills is a pyroclastic volcano. Instead of burning lava, it blasts out huge columns of immensely hot ash, gas, and rock, which collapse and rush from the volcano, destroying everything in their path.

Column of gas and ash...

Team of scientists

There were four of us at the observatory, all qualified scientists but with different roles to play. The director liaises with the civil authorities in Montserrat. Then there was myself and another volcanologist, and a seismologist. The seismologist is in charge of monitoring the movement of magma shifting beneath the surface. This movement causes earthquakes. Not the big ones you get in places like California and Turkey, but fairly small ones caused by magma forcing its way through cracks in brittle rock. As the magma rises to a shallow level, it releases tell-tale gases and scientists can detect tremor—a sign that an eruption is underway. The seismologist is in charge of putting out seismometers—instruments to measure the force and size of the tremor. The information is sent back to the observatory by radio waves. Then the seismologist goes through the data and processes it using special software to look at the waveforms and the frequency of the earthquakes. He then tries to interpret what's going on within the volcano.

...racing downward to the sea

Predicting danger

Monitoring a volcano like the one in Montserrat means working a seven-day week much of the time. You have to be on the alert continually, because people are living so close to it. We had to be able to forecast an eruption and evacuate people living nearby. By monitoring it closely we have built up a picture of what's happening underground and the cycles the volcano goes through. We've learned to forecast not just eruptions, but the likely path of the pyroclastic flow—an avalanche of hot gas, ash, and lava fragments that explodes from the volcano.

Different types of lava

Soufrière Hills is a very different type of volcano from the kind you see in Hawaii—where I have also worked. That kind of volcano doesn't have such large explosions because of the low viscosity, or runniness, of the basalt lava. It's a little like comparing oil and water. Hawaiian lava is so fluid that gases can escape very easily, so the most common type of activity is very slow, but heavy lava flows. At Soufrière Hills, the lava is andesite, which is much more viscous and sticky, like syrup, so gases are trapped. Immense pressure builds up inside the volcano, then the gases and debris force their way out.

Volcanologists at work

The two of us were in charge of all of the other monitoring. There are many ways to do this. One was visual observation. There was a helipad at the observatory and an important part of the day was to go up in a helicopter with cameras and video cameras and fly around the volcano summit to see what was happening. It was exciting—certainly my favorite part of the day! We had the helicopter for a few hours each morning, so we would use it to go to sites where instruments were installed to check that they were working properly.

Incandescent trails seen at night

GROUNDWORK
The volcanologists use a gadget called a theodolite to survey the surface of the lava dome that's built up in the crater.

FLYING EYE
Marie takes her daily trip in the helicopter, flying above the volcano to look directly down at the summit, taking photographs and measuring gases.

"We flew around the volcano summit in a helicopter. It was exciting— my favorite part of the day"

Checking the gas

Another important way we monitored the volcano was by looking at its gas emissions. By flying through the volcanic plumes, we could measure the composition and amount of gas coming from the volcano. For that we used an instrument called a spectrometer. One of the main gases we measured was sulfur dioxide, which is a gas you don't usually find in Earth's atmosphere. Sulfur dioxide is produced by power plants and pollution, so clouds often contain it. But generally there's none in the background air, so a sudden increase in the gas is easy to measure. Volcanoes are a major producer of sulfur dioxide. We flew directly underneath the volcanic plumes and used an ultra-violet spectrometer to measure the amount of sulfur dioxide in a section of the plume. Then using the plume's speed—how fast the plume is blowing away from the volcano—we could work out how much gas is being emitted every hour or even every minute. An increase in sulfur dioxide in the air was a clear indication that things were heating up inside the volcano.

Getting grounded

Sometimes the pilots won't fly, but that is because of the ash more than the gases. The ash gets into the helicopter engines and is very fine grained. The high temperatures within the helicopter engines can melt the ash particles so the engine becomes clogged. That's a major danger for aircraft worldwide. In Montserrat when we have very big explosions, the eruption columns would rise up several miles high. I think we had an ash column up to 50,000 ft (15 km) several times throughout the eruption. Antigua, the big island next door, is a very popular tourist destination—when there's an eruption, the airport there is closed and aircraft are diverted away from the island.

MEASURING ASH
Marie describes and measures ash fall. A maximum of 5 in (12 cm) fell on July 12–13, 2003, right after a large lava dome collapse and a series of explosive eruptions. That happens about once every two years.

Monitoring the ash

We also went out by jeep every day to check equipment stationed around the island and monitor the ash fall. We had a solar-powered gas monitoring installation in an area called Lovers' Lane on the outskirts of the deserted capital town, Plymouth. There was a spectrometer and a rotating system that scanned the volcanic plume to measure sulfur dioxide output from the volcano. Examining the grain-size and volume of ash around the island helped us to reconstruct the volcanic activity. I went around the island looking at different ash sections

Marie with gas monitoring equipment

Measuring ash by a villa pool

describe the layers and measure their thickness. Beside swimming pools was quite a convenient place to look, since it's at ground. Most of the tourist villas have swimming pools.

DUSTY PICKUP
The people of Montserrat are used to living with volcanic dust—in some areas, it covers everything. The amount of dust varies depending on how active the volcano is.

Cycles of activity

Over the last decade the volcano has gone through several regular cycles. As it becomes more active, the lava builds up into a dome within the volcano crater, and gets higher, until it collapses. The volcano is then quieter for a few months, before the whole cycle starts over again. It's when a major dome collapse is on the way that the volcano is most dangerous, because the collapse may result in gas, rock, and ash being erupted. In this event, the director advises the civil authorities to evacuate threatened areas. The enforcement of the exclusion zone is carried out by the police and the army under instructions from the government.

Evacuation calls

Exclusion zones are based on where pyroclastic flows might go and pyroclastic surges—the part of the flow that can go uphill. So far we have come up with a kind of line north of Old Towne, which we think is the most likely target. This is on the south of the island. A few local people live in the danger zone but most of the houses are vacation homes owned by North Americans and Europeans who come here for the winter. The locals call them "snow birds"! Tourism is the main economy for Montserrat, and looking after the villas is one of the biggest source of income for many of the locals— the cleaning ladies who clean the houses, the cooks, the groundskeepers, the swimming pool cleaners. The eruptions have affected tourism and hit Montserrat really hard financially.

People of Montserrat

The volcano has also taken lives, though the only fatalities since this eruption started were the 26 people who died in 1997. They had gone back into the exclusion zone —the area around the volcano— after it had been evacuated. The police were guarding several checkpoints, but people wanted to go back in to check their houses, or their farms—many had crops they wanted to tend. They went back, volcanic activity built up, and they were unlucky. There were suddenly lots of explosions and pyroclastic flows. Back then, it was all so new and the activity increased so quickly—at a rate that was really unprecedented in the previous two years. Now we all have a much better sense of what the volcano is capable of.

LIFE IN THE SHADOW
People who live on the margins of the dangerous flows are familiar with the process, so they know that when the volcano gets active they will probably be evacuated to the north of the island. When it's over they can move back.

THE CLOCK TOWER IN PLYMOUTH
Montserrat's capital city, Plymouth, was abandoned in 1997 after it was buried under ash during the largest eruption. Now, the top of the clock tower is all that can be seen of the once attractive and thriving town. Brades, in the north, has become the business center for the island.

"In the field, we kept in constant contact with the observatory as the volcano is not totally predictable"

Close to the danger zone

We walked down into the danger zone fairly regularly. There's a gas spectrometer installation on the west coast, south of Plymouth. We walked through the old town, and past the old buried airport on the east, and farther south when activity was low. That could be a fairly dangerous area. It has been hit by pyroclastic flow. When in the field we had twoway radios and cell phones to keep in constant contact with the observatory. The volcano is not totally predictable, so we wouldn't go there if the lava dome was big or if there was a lot of pyroclastic activity going on. We mainly went after a large dome collapse, so the buildup of ash and volcanic material had gone from the crater.

Collecting samples

We went to collect samples and look at deposits. Pyroclastic flow deposits were still hot, so we had to wear heavy gloves to handle samples and try not to stand on the lava as the rocks and ash could easily melt our boots. We had to wear heat-resistant suits called hot suits. There are different types of suits. The ones used in Montserrat are heat-resistant coveralls—orange fabric that's chemically treated so it won't burst into flames. In Etna, in Italy, and Kilauea, in Hawaii, you wear silver reflective suits, since these deflect the heat away more effectively. There the runny basalt lava is much hotter—it can get up to temperatures of around 2,192°F (1,200°C), so you can catch fire just by getting close to lava. In Montserrat, we are talking about temperatures of up to 1,472°F (800°C).

In the lab

We used to shovel deposits into a bucket, take them back to the observatory, and then wait for them to cool before putting them into sample bags. We've built up this huge database of samples taken all the way through the eruption from different deposits on different days, at different times in the activity cycle, and so on. This collection provides a resource for people working at universities, like I am now, who can ask the observatory for samples to analyze. Examining the samples is important, but it's not done in real-time, on a day-to-day basis while working at the observatory. Instead, it is done by researchers at universities who have access to special instruments for microanalysis. It is exciting being out there, but when you are based out in the field, you have limited equipment, facilities, and resources to study the crystals within the samples. Magma rises from Earth's mantle layer and

DWINDLING POPULATION

The Soufrière Hills Volcano is still active and there are still evacuations at dangerous times. Two-thirds of the island is now covered with ash and uninhabited. The remaining islanders have moved to the north of Montserrat.

crystallizes as it loses gases and cools. The composition of the magma changes as it rises through the crust. So when we look at rocks that have erupted at the surface, we can actually look at the history of the magma that formed them.

Follow-up work

Usually scientists based at a university have just a couple of field trips a year—a mad, crazy time trying to collect data to take back. This keeps them going for six months or so while they look at the data and work out what's going on. I went directly from Montserrat to Hawaii to work at the observatory there. Now I am back in the UK and in a good position, where I have an incredible amount of data and I can sit and think quietly about everything.

Types of Expert

THERE ARE MANY FIELDS of geoscience, each requiring specialized skills. Geoscientists explore how Earth works and do vital work monitoring eruptions and earthquakes, searching for valuable raw materials, conserving natural resources, and researching climate change.

SEISMOLOGIST

A powerful earthquake can shatter buildings and roads, causing disruption and loss of life. Effective warning systems for an earthquake—or a tsunami—are important. A seismologist studies earthquakes, using sensitive instruments called seismometers to measure the seismic waves produced by movements in the Earth's crust. A quake's magnitude (how much energy it releases) is measured on the Richter scale, ranging from under 2 for a microearthquake, to 8 or above. The Modified Mercalli scale is used to measure damage on the ground.

EARTHQUAKE RESEARCH
Seismic observatories gather data on earth tremors from fault lines and volcanoes. This data is used to try and forecast future earthquake hazards.

SEISMOGRAPH
A seismograph is a device with a weighted pen that records the tremors produced by a quake in a zigzag line, called a seismogram.

LIVING FOSSIL
The Wollemi pine was known only from Jurassic fossils until some living trees were discovered in 1994 in Australia.

EXTRACTION OF DNA
DNA extracted from pulp inside the tooth of a frozen specimen of an extinct American mastodon is compared with that of a modern elephant.

PALEONTOLOGIST

Pick up a piece of stone on a beach or by a rock outcrop and you just might find a fossil. The job of the paleontologist is to collect, identify, and study fossils—the remains or traces of animals and plants preserved in rock. These range from tiny specks of pollen to the footprints of giant dinosaurs. They provide vital clues about how environments and life on Earth have evolved. Equipped with a geological map and hammer, collecting bag, and notebook, a paleontologist is part of that investigation and uses fossils to give a relative age to the rocks in which they are found. Preparing specimens and reconstructing fossil fragments into complete specimens can take months, even years, of highly skilled and careful work back in the museum or laboratory. The fossils are then labeled and stored where they can be used by experts for research.

VOLCANOLOGIST

As the world's population increases, more people live with the ever-present threat of active volcanoes. A volcanologist researches how volcanoes work, to help predict eruptions so that preventive measures can be planned. This involves monitoring active craters and vents, sampling lava and measuring gases, and interpeting data in the laboratory.

Sensitive equipment inside craters, such as that of Vesuvius, is linked by satellite in a global network, so that news of an eruption or a tsunami can reach threatened locations with the utmost speed.

HOT WORK
Surveying lava fields near active volcanoes requires protective clothing, very tough boots, and breathing equipment to protect the lungs from hot and poisonous gases.

cinder cone

vent

mineral spring

ground water

main conduit

steeply sloping cone consisting of numerous layers of ash and lava

secondary conduit

magma reservoir

LOOKING INSIDE
This cross-section model of a volcano shows key features studied by a volcanologist. With each new eruption, magma (molten rock) is forced up through the central conduit and cools and hardens on the surface, adding a new layer to the cone. By sampling the layered ashes and lava, a volcanologist can gather important information about previous eruptions.

SPELEOLOGIST

The network of caves and waterways winding their way through the Earth's sedimentary rocks are a rewarding field of study for anyone interested in geology and archeology. The speleologist, or cave explorer, needs to be physically fit and adventurous! Cave surveying can involve going deep underground and squeezing through narrow passages, so speleologists have to travel light, wearing protective helmets and carrying only essential hand tools, such as a flashlight, camera, compass, and tape. Diving skills help, too, since many caves are flooded.

YUCATAN CAVES
A diver explores a sinkhole, called a cenote, in Mexico's Yucatan peninsula. The area is honey-combed with these collapsed caverns, formed as acidic ground water dissolved the limestone bedrock.

COSQUER CAVES
Stenciled handprints 27,000 years old were found in a cave discovered by diver Henri Cosquer on the French coast. The entrance is a tunnel now 120 ft (37 m) below sea level.

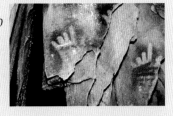

PETROLOGIST

Petrology takes its name from *petra* (Greek for "rock") and is the study of rocks, including the major types—igneous, sedimentary, and metamorphic. A petrologist's job is to research the composition of rocks, and to discover how, where, and when they were formed. Some of the work is carried out in the field, exploring rock formations, collecting samples, and making detailed notes and maps. Back in the laboratory, rock samples are examined and analyzed using specialized equipment. Experimental petrologists test rocks by subjecting them to heat and pressure in furnaces, to simulate conditions deep in Earth's crust, where igneous and metamorphic rocks are formed.

Petrologist Sally Gibson examines rock samples in an outcrop in central Brazil. These will be sliced into thin sections and examined carefully under a microscope.

MINERALOGIST

Each type of rock is made up of a particular collection of minerals. A mineralogist studies Earth's naturally occurring minerals, from spectacular gemstones to radioactive ores. He or she may work in university research, for governments or mining companies doing exploration work, or as a curator in a museum. There are over 4,000 kinds of mineral, with new ones being discovered every year. Some can be identified easily by their physical and chemical properties, but laboratory equipment is needed to pin down more challenging examples. Machines called electron probe microanlyzers and X-ray spectrometers bombard specimens with electrons to reveal the atomic structure of their crystals.

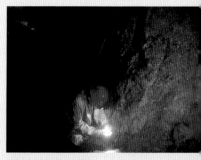

DIAMOND RUSH
In 1985, geologist Charles Fipke discovered pipes of volcanic rock containing diamond deposits in the Canadian Arctic. Mining companies soon staked their claims.

ARGYLE MINE
This vast strip mine on the Kimberley Plateau, West Australia, is the world's largest diamond producer. The deposits, formed between 1.6 and 1.9 billion years ago, were discovered in 1976. Rocks containing industrial and gem quality pink diamonds are blasted and hauled out by truck for processing.

GLACIOLOGIST

The world's polar ice sheets and mountain glaciers have helped to shape our landscape. They also hold clues to climates in the past. Glaciologists study these ice sheets, and their work takes them to some of the most remote places on Earth. Fieldwork can involve several months spent away from home in an Antarctic field station, with trips out over the ice to collect samples and monitor the ice cap from year to year for changes in its growth, flow, and melting. These core samples are a valuable source of information and are kept for years in cold storage centers. Frozen evidence of levels of carbon dioxide, one of the gases responsible for global warming, is currently an important area of research.

CLIMATE CHANGE
Ice cores from the Antarctic ice sheet contain air bubbles that provide data about the atmosphere at the time the bubbles became trapped.

CE CORE DRILLING
sing a portable drilling device, glaciologists pull ut long sections of compacted ice and snow, called res, from the ice sheet. These contain data that elps to build up a picture of the climate in the past.

METEOR EXPERT

ome geologists study rocks from space that land on arth. These meteorites range from huge objects that reate vast craters as they smash into the ground, to ore frequent showers of tiny fragments. Research an involve expeditions to deserts or ice sheets, here specimens are easier to find, or work in a useum analyzing and classifying samples. Meteorites provide aluable evidence about the other rocky bodies in the solar ystem and about its origin and formation.

METEORITE
Most meteorites consist mainly of iron, with an outer crust produced by melting as they pass through Earth's atmosphere.

BARRINGER CRATER
In the Arizona desert the impact of a meteor that fell nearly 50,000 years ago created a bowl-shaped crater with a diameter of over 4,000 ft (1 km).

Tools and Techniques

EQUIPMENT USED BY GEOSCIENTISTS ranges from portable tools
that can be tucked into a backpack to sophisticated electron
microscopes and computers linked globally by satellites.
However, most geologists will have spent part of their
training in the field, breaking up rocks with a sturdy
geological hammer and using a pocket-sized hand lens
to examine the pieces for minerals or fossils.

circular
stand

NOTEBOOK
*During field work, geologists make
detailed on-the-spot notes, recording
the rock's location, its characteristics,
and the type of strata where it is found.*

TAPE MEASURE
*Accurate measurements are taken and
recorded in the notebook, so that the rock
or fossil locality can be found again on
subsequent visits.*

THEODOLITE
*A theodolite is an optical
instrument, consisting of a
telescope on a tripod, for taking
precise measurements of
angles, distances, and
heights in a landscape.
Geoscientists use
theodolites for mapping
and surveying, and for
monitoring changes in
volcanic areas and
ice sheets.*

**DIGITAL
THERMOMETER**
*As magma rises inside
a volcano, it releases hot
gases through volcanic vents
called fumeroles. Changes in
temperature near a fumerole help indicate
whether a volcano is about to erupt.*

BATHYMETRIC MAPPING

A depth measurement system called bathymetry combines the techniques of echo-sounding and satellite global positioning systems (GPS) to create contour maps of the seabed. This color image shows the geological features of the Hawaiian Island chain and the surrounding ocean floor.

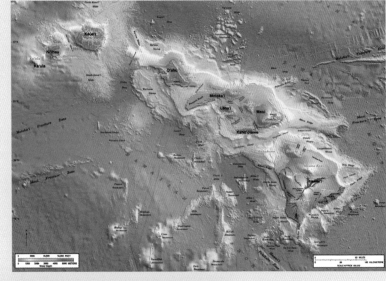

telescope eyepiece

leveling screws

IMPACT CRATER RESEARCH

Experiments with models of past geological events provide valuable data for researchers. This aluminum pellet strikes a sand target at high speed, creating a small impact crater and throwing up debris. The experiment simulates the arrival of a large meteorite from space.

SUBMERSIBLE

The submersible Pisces V takes scientists as deep as 6,300 ft (2,000 m) to observe and film the Loihi Seamount, a new volcanic island emerging as the Hawaiian islands move slowly over a hot-spot in the Pacific tectonic plate.

sampling arm

divers preparing Pisces V for a dive

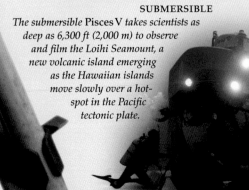

adjustable legs

Hall of Fame

LOUIS RODOLPHE AGASSIZ

1807-1873

JOB: Glaciologist

COUNTRY: Switzerland

Louis Agassiz was a world expert on fossil fish, but he achieved even greater fame for his theory of Ice Ages. He studied glaciers, and noticed the presence of glacial features, such as U-shaped valleys and giant boulders called erratics, in places far from where glaciers then existed. This led him to believe that a vast ice sheet had once stretched around the globe from the North Pole to the Mediterranean Sea. In 1846, Agassiz emigrated to the US, where he became Professor of Zoology and Geology at Harvard University and had a highly successful career.

Louis Rodolphe Agassiz

GEORGIUS AGRICOLA

1494-1555

JOB: Physician/mineralogist

COUNTRY: Germany

Georg Bauer wrote under the pen name Georgius Agricola. He worked as a doctor in the mining town of Joachimsthal, Czech Republic, where he was able to watch mining processes at close quarters. In 1555 he published a book classifying minerals and describing how they were extracted. The careful observations in *De Re Metallica* (*On the Nature of Metals*) are superbly illustrated with woodcuts that are of great historical interest today. Other books covered fossils and the origins of rocks, mountains, earthquakes, and volcanoes.

LUIS AND WALTER ALVAREZ

1911-1988 (LUIS) 1940- (WALTER)

JOB: Physicist (Luis)
Geologist (Walter)

COUNTRY: US

Father and son Luis and Walter Alvarez discovered high levels of the rare chemical element iridium in sedimentary rock strata in Gubbio, northern Italy. The age of the rocks coincided with the extinction of the dinosaurs 65 million years ago. The Alvarez team proposed that the impact of a giant asteroid from space caused a massive dust cloud, with high levels of iridium. The resulting drop in global temperatures wiped out the dinosaurs and many other species of animals and plants in a massive extinction event.

Luis and Walter Alvarez

HUGO BENIOFF

1899-1968

JOB: Seismologist

COUNTRY: US

Hugo Benioff was a multitalented inventor who designed sensitive equipment to measure shaking and stretching in Earth's crust. He began his career as an astronomer, but changed to seismology and became a world expert on the seismic waves produced by

Hugo Benioff

earthquakes. They originate deep down where continental and oceanic tectonic plates collide. Benioff showed that these deep earthquakes were the result of ocean crust being subducted (descending) below the continents.

SIR WILLIAM HENRY BRAGG & SIR WILLIAM LAWRENCE BRAGG

1862–1942, 1890–1971

JOB: Physicists

COUNTRY: UK

At 25, Lawrence Bragg was the youngest person ever to win a Nobel Prize, shared in 1915 with his father, Australian-born William Henry Bragg. Together they pioneered the study of crystals using X-ray diffraction, a technique that measured the reflections of X-ray waves from crystal faces. To do this, Bragg senior developed and refined the X-ray spectrometer, while his son produced Bragg's Law (1912), showing how X-rays reveal the atomic structure of crystals. This science, crystallography, plays a vital part in the study of minerals.

Sir William Lawrence

MAURICE EWING

1906–1974

JOB: Geophysicist/oceanographer

COUNTRY: US

Texan Maurice "Doc" Ewing did pioneering work in plate tectonics. He studied the ocean floor, leading over 50 underwater expeditions and developing new exploration equipment. He demonstrated that the ocean crust is thinner than continental crust. He also showed that along the Mid-Atlantic Ridge, Earth's crust is being pulled apart by plate tectonic forces, forming a rift.

GEORGES-LOUIS LECLERC (COMTE DE BUFFON)

1707–1788

JOB: Naturalist

COUNTRY: France

Aristocrat Georges-Louis Leclerc was an avid natural historian, mathematician, astronomer, and an influential writer. He produced a summary in 44 volumes of all that was then known about the natural world. He also did experiments with cooling iron, which led him to the revolutionary conclusion that Earth was at least 75,000 years old, far older than what was then accepted by the Catholic Church.

INGE LEHMANN

1883–1993

JOB: Geophysicist

COUNTRY: Denmark

When Inge Lehmann began her career, there were few women geologists, and even fewer Danish seismologists. In 1928, she became the first head of the seismology department in the Royal Danish Geodetic Institute. In a scientific paper in 1936, titled simply "P," she published exciting new research about the mysterious center of Earth. By studying the patterns of seismic P waves, she had discovered that there is a liquid outer core surrounding a solid inner core.

JULES MARCOU

1824–1898

JOB: Geologist

COUNTRY: Switzerland

Jules Marcou made his name by producing one of the first geological maps of North America in 1853. As research, he had spent several years traveling around the US and Canada. In 1861, he published a geological map of the world.

Jules Marcou

MOTONORI MATUYAMA

1884–1958

JOB: Geophysicist

COUNTRY: Japan

In 1929, Motonori Matuyama published his extraordinary discovery about Earth's magnetism. In basalt lavas, the north and south poles had been reversed and reversed again, which suggested that Earth's magnetic field had flipped many times over the past two million years. Measuring and mapping these magnetic reversals has helped develop the idea that crustal plates have moved over time—a process known as plate tectonics.

DAN MCKENZIE

1942–

JOB: Geophysicist

COUNTRY: UK

A key figure in the story of plate tectonics is a Cambridge professor of geophysics, Dan McKenzie. By the late 1960s his work had helped to gain acceptance for this great unifying theory, which explains how whole continents are moved slowly around Earth's surface, with oceans being created and destroyed in the process. Since then, he has done important research on the formation of sedimentary basins, and on the geology of Venus and Mars.

ANDRIJA MOHOROVICIC

1857–1936

JOB: Seismologist/meteorologist

COUNTRY: Croatia

The Moho Discontinuity marks the boundary between Earth's mantle and the crust and ranges from 3 miles (5 km) below the oceans to 45 miles (70 km)

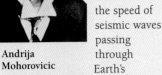

Andrija
Mohorovicic

beneath high mountains. It is named after Andrija Mohorovicic, who discovered differences in the speed of seismic waves passing through Earth's interior. By measuring the waves produced by a large earthquake in Croatia in 1909, he discovered a sharp contact between the surface crustal rocks and the denser upper mantle.

LAWRENCE MORLEY

1920–

JOB: Geophysics

COUNTRY: Canada

Lawrence Morley's name is linked with those of British geologists Frederick Vine and Drummond Matthews in studies of magnetic reversals in the ocean floor. Their mapping work revealed rocks arranged in alternating strips parallel to the Mid-Atlantic Ridge, with matching strips on both sides of the ridge. In 1962, Morley, Vine, and Matthews proposed that magma emerging from the center of the ridge was pushing the plates apart to form new crust. This process, known as sea-floor spreading, plays a crucial part in plate tectonics.

SIR RODERICK IMPEY MURCHISON

1782–1871

JOB: Geologist

COUNTRY: Scotland

After a career in the army during the Napoleonic wars, Murchison became interested in geology and by 1831 was president of the Royal Geological Society of London, England. During a very active career, he studied the geological strata of England and Wales, defining a new period, or system, called the Silurian, covering the time from 30 to 440 million years ago. He also did important work on Cambrian and Devonian systems with leading geologist Cambridge Adam Sedgwick and traveled to Russia between 1840 and 1844 to establish the Permian system.

Clair
Patterson

CLAIR CAMERON PATTERSON

1922–1995

JOB: Geochemist

COUNTRY: US

Clair Patterson developed the uranium-lead method for determining the age of igneous rock. This type of radiometric dating uses knowledge of how long uranium and lead isotopes take to decay. Using data collected from the Canyon Diablo meteorite—which fell in Arizona between 20,000 and 40,000 years ago—Patterson calculated a reliable age for the Earth's formation some 4.55 billion years ago.

PLINY THE ELDER

CE 23–79

JOB: Naturalist

COUNTRY: Italy

Pliny was a hard-working Roman naturalist who studied and listed all the active volcanoes then known. In 79 CE, he was commanding a Roman fleet when Vesuvius began to erupt, and after sailing closer to rescue friends, he collapsed and died. Meanwhile, his nephew, Pliny the Younger (62–c. 114 CE), watched the eruption and wrote a clear and accurate description of the event. The eruption subsequently engulfed the towns of Pompeii and Herculaneum. Large explosive volcanic eruptions with large columns of gas have since been called Plinian eruptions.

HAROUN TAZIEFF

1914–1998

JOB: Volcanologist

COUNTRY: Belgium

Volcanologist, photographer, and film director Haroun Tazieff brought the drama of eruptions and lava flows to millions of television viewers, through his world-famous documentaries. Born in Warsaw to Russian-Polish parents, he eventually settled in Belgium where he graduated as a geologist in 1944. He was appointed to the French cabinet as secretary of state for the prevention of natural disasters in 1984.

WILLIAM THOMSON LORD KELVIN

1824–1907

JOB: Physicist

COUNTRY: UK

William Thomson was born in Belfast, Northern Ireland, and educated in Scotland. He was an outstanding scientist, who gave his name to the Kelvin scale of temperature measurement and estimated the age of Earth. He believed that it had once been a "red-hot globe" and calculated that it must have taken 100 million years to cool to its present temperature, later shortening this to 40 million years. In 1892, he was made a peer to honor his

Haroun Tazieff in the field

achievements, becoming Baron Kelvin of Largs.

ALFRED LOTHAR WEGENER

1880–1930

JOB: Meteorologist/ geophysicist

COUNTRY: Germany

Alfred Wegener made several expeditions to Arctic Greenland, the last of which would claim his life. However, he has achieved lasting fame for proposing, in 1915, the idea that the positions of the continents are not fixed, but have moved around slowly on the globe in a process called continental drift. His evidence for this included the fact that outlines of eastern South America and West Africa fit neatly if pushed together, rock strata matched on each side of the oceans, and fossils of the same animals were also separated by oceans. Wegener's ideas were ridiculed at the time, but they were later proved to be correct. By the 1960s, geologists had an explanation for the changing positions of continents and oceans—the theory of plate tectonics.

ABRAHAM GOTTLOB WERNER

1749–1817

JOB: Mineralogist

COUNTRY: Germany

Abraham Werner's boyhood interest in rocks and minerals developed into a career in mineralogy, when in 1775 he was given a position in Freiberg Mining Academy as a teacher, inspector, and mineral curator. He proved to be an exceptional lecturer, attracting students from all over Europe. Werner was a pioneer of stratigraphy—he demonstrated that rocks were laid down in a particular order, now known as a succession. At a time when geologists were disagreeing about the exact origins of rocks, Werner was a Neptunist. He believed that all rocks were deposited under water, at a time when Earth was completely covered by oceans.

Alfred Wegener

2
ACTIVITIES

Have you got what it takes to be a geologist? Find out how much you know and hone your skills with our challenging activities.

Which expert are you?

Inspired by the exciting work of the rock and mineral experts you've read about, you are set on a career in the field—but which branch of geology is for you? Try our fun flowchart and find out!

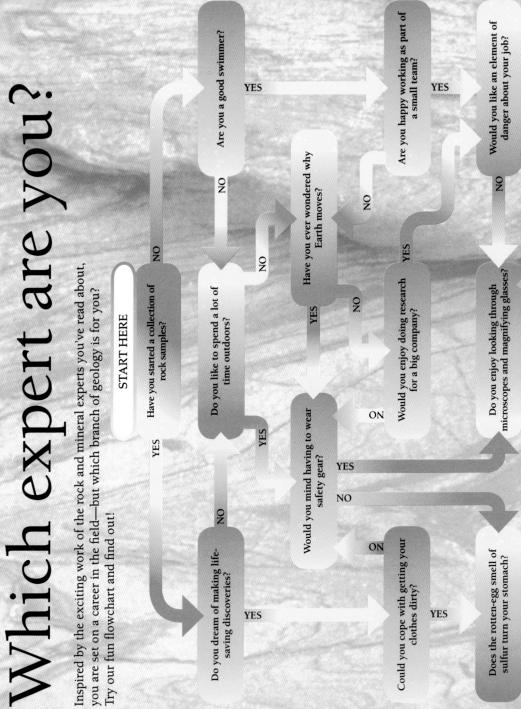

START HERE

Have you started a collection of rock samples?

NO

YES

Do you dream of making life-saving discoveries?

NO

YES

Are you a good swimmer?

YES

NO

Do you like to spend a lot of time outdoors?

YES

NO

Have you ever wondered why Earth moves?

YES

NO

Are you happy working as part of a small team?

YES

NO

Would you like an element of danger about your job?

YES

NO

Would you enjoy doing research for a big company?

YES

NO

Would you mind having to wear safety gear?

YES

NO

Do you enjoy looking through microscopes and magnifying glasses?

YES

Could you cope with getting your clothes dirty?

NO

YES

Does the rotten-egg smell of sulfur turn your stomach?

NO

Are you good at solving sudoku number puzzles?

YES

NO

Do you long to explore somewhere not many people go?

YES

NO

Are you scared of being in confined spaces?

NO

YES

Are you fascinated by the destructive force of magma?

YES

NO

Are you scared of heights?

YES

NO

Could you spend hours analyzing chemical properties of samples?

NO

YES

Do you enjoy studying graphs and charts?

NO

YES

SPELEOLOGIST

You're an avid adventurer, always on the go, and the idea of diving to a hidden underwater cave fills you with excitement. Keep in shape and do your research so you'll stay safe!

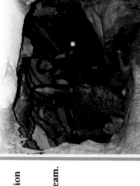

MINERALOGIST

You've already amassed a collection of rock and mineral samples and made methodical field notes. Being able to examine them with high-tech lab equipment for oil companies or other exploration businesses would be your dream.

SEISMOLOGIST

You love research, you're good at math, and you are fascinated by the Earth's power. It all points to seismology, and warning populations about coming quakes.

VOLCANOLOGIST

You are not fazed by facing dangers and working in conditions others would find unbearable, and you long to uncover the secrets hidden deep within the Earth's mantle.

Link the rock

LEVEL 1

How long did it take you?

☐ 10 mins: Expert

☐ 15 mins: Knowledgable

☐ 20 mins: Beginner.

Rock is everywhere! There are buildings and historic landmarks all over the world made of it—some man-made and some formed by geological processes. Can you write down which country each famous site is in? Then match the rock to the photo.

 You can write on a blackboard with a piece of the White Cliffs of Dover. See *Eyewitness Rocks & Minerals* for further help.

Marble

☐

Flint

☐

Basaltic Lava

☐

Limestone

☐

Red Sandstone

☐

Phonolitic Lava

☐

Taj Mahal ....

2. Grand Canyon ....

White Cliffs of Dover ....

4. Pyramids at Giza ....

Devil's Tower ....

6. Giant's Causeway ....

All that glitters

The beauty of minerals comes from their color and shape.
Gemstones are naturally occurring minerals that may look
dull when mined but stunning when cut and polished. Ca
you match the uncut stones to the polished ones? Write
the correct numbers in the boxes.

HOW LONG
DID IT TAKE YOU?

☐ 10 mins:
Expert

☐ 15 mins:
Knowledgable

☐ 20 mins:
Beginner

UNCUT STONES

1. Zircon

See *Eyewitness Rocks &
Minerals* if you want to
shine.

3. Opal

2. Ruby

6. Tourmaline

4. Diamond

5. Emerald

7. Turquoise

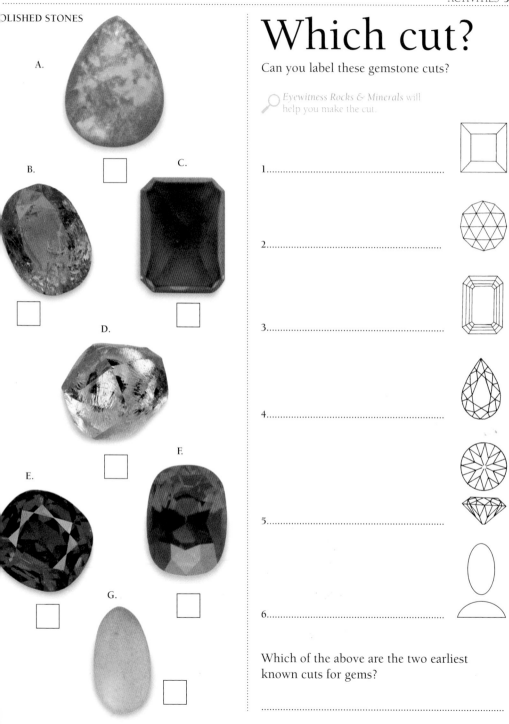

POLISHED STONES

A.

B.

C.

D.

E.

F.

G.

Which cut?

Can you label these gemstone cuts?

Eyewitness Rocks & Minerals will help you make the cut.

1..

2..

3..

4..

5..

6..

Which of the above are the two earliest known cuts for gems?

....

LEVEL
2

Tool test

For centuries, rock has been a useful material for making tools, from domestic and agricultural implements to weapons. Can you guess what these objects are? Check your answers in *Eyewitness Rocks & Minerals*.

HOW LONG
DID IT TAKE YOU?

☐ 10 mins:
Expert

☐ 15 mins:
Knowledgable

☐ 20 mins:
Beginner

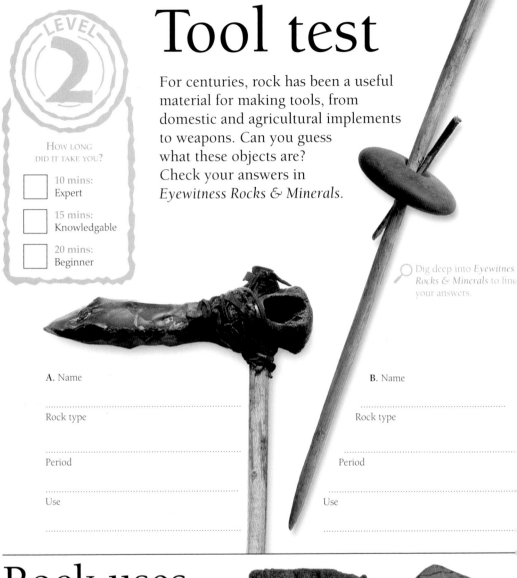

○ Dig deep into *Eyewitness Rocks & Minerals* to find your answers.

A. Name

....

Rock type

....

Period

....

Use

....

B. Name

....

Rock type

....

Period

....

Use

....

Rock uses

What uses can you find for each of these rocks?

○ Think up some ideas of your own and then use *Eyewitness Rocks & Minerals* to check your answers.

1. Coal

2. Slate

C. Name

Rock type

Period

Use

D. Name

Rock type

Period

Use

E. Name

Rock type

Period

Use

3. Cinnabar,
mercury ore

4. Lapis

Write the uses here.

1

2

3

4

Rock groups

Rocks are grouped into different types, according to the way they are formed. The main types are sedimentary, igneous, and metamorphic. Sort these sample rocks into their correct groups by writing one of the three types next to each rock.

LEVEL 2

How long
did it take you?

☐ 10 mins:
Expert

☐ 15 mins:
Knowledgable

☐ 20 mins:
Beginner

1. Schist

....

2. Granite

....

3. Sandstone

....

5. Obsidian

....

4. Marble

....

6. Flint

....

You will need *Eyewitness Rocks & Minerals* and your Profile Cards to complete these two tasks.

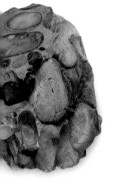

. Conglomerate

8. Gabbro

....

. Limestone

....

10. Gneiss

....

Label it

Volanic rocks belong to the same family as igneous rocks. Name the ones below, then circle the odd-one-out.

A. Name

....

B. Name

....

C. Name

....

D. Name

....

Shape spotters

Minerals crystallize into geometrical shapes and are organized, according to their symmetry, into six main groups or crystal systems. Use your Profile Cards to work out which system each of these minerals belongs to.

How long
did it take you?

☐ 10 mins:
Expert

☐ 15 mins:
Knowledgable

☐ 20 mins:
Beginner

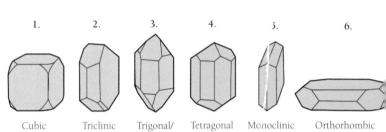

1.	2.	3.	4.	5.	6.
Cubic	Triclinic	Trigonal/ Hexagonal	Tetragonal	Monoclinic	Orthorhombic

A. Olivine

....

B. Lazulite

....

C. Zircon

D. Azurite

E. Barite

....

F. Galena

G. Quartz

H. Albite

J. Uraninite

I. Calcite

K. Microcline

If you feel like an expert now, try answering the questions without looking at your Profile Cards or *Eyewitness Rocks & Minerals*, then use them to check how you've done.

L. Cassiterite

EXPERTS' LOG

3

It's time to get organized and start your own research. Check out the simple tools that every budding expert needs. Your career in geology starts here!

At the museum

What to take
- Notebook
- Pencil
- Camera

• Many museums show collections of local rocks, minerals, and fossils. It's a chance to see a large range close up, make notes, and draw them. You may also be able to compare minerals as they are dug up and then cut and polished.

• Look on the display cards for further information and write here or keep a log in a notebook or scrapbook on where each type of rock is found.

• Major geological sites and National Parks have visitor centers where you can learn about the geology of an area. Mining areas, cave complexes, and volcano sites may also have displays and even a tour. See page 68 of Eyewitness Rocks & Minerals for good places to visit.

• Aside from collections, look for exhibits revealing Earth's structure. You may not be able to visit the Grand Canyon, but you could see displays of the different strata, or layers, in Earth's crust.

• Some museums allow you to take photographs, but not all! If not, visit the museum store and look for postcards of your favorite fossils or exhibits and add those to your notebook or scrapbook. They may also sell rock and mineral samples to add to your collection.

Natural history museums are exciting places to visit. Some have installations showing how volcanoes or earthquakes work or cross-sections of Earth's crust.

In the field

GATHERING SPECIMENS

Tools to take
- Notebook
- Pencil
- Soft brush to dust away dirt
- Bag or box
- Paper to wrap your finds in
- Camera

• Field work is an important part of a geologist's job. Perhaps your parents or teacher will organize a trip to visit a place famous for its rocks or minerals, or to a local site to see what geology is common in your area.

• Draw sketches or take photographs of all of your finds and make a note of where you found them. Label the samples and the date of your trip.

• Without field notes, your samples are of little scientific value! Use the space here to make detailed notes on your finds or keep a log in your notebook to carry on each trip.

• Try to identify your rock or mineral. Do you know if the rock is sedimentary, metamorphic, or igneous? Check the color, grain size, and texture. Does it match any of the profiles on your cards?

• Stay safe! Don't wander off alone, or go near cliff edges or quarries. You may be asked to wear safety goggles and hardhats near rock faces.

• Geologists respect the land and collecting is not allowed at many protected sites. Check before you collect, and don't destroy the environment. Always ask permission to go on private land.

Whether you are out in your backyard, on the beach or near a volcano, keep an eye out for interesting rocks and minerals and start your own collection.

....

....

....

....

....

....

....

....

Research

WHERE TO LOOK

Books

Still an essential resource for any expert. Aside from illustrated guides detailing individual rocks and minerals, you can look up the places you have visited on your field trips to find out more about their geology and identify any specimens you saw.

The media

Geologists keep an eye on the news and read scientific journals to find out what volcanoes are going off, where earthquakes take place, and details of new geological discoveries. Record your research into the latest finds or events, noting dates and location. Or take clippings to place here or file in your scrapbook or log.

The web

There are many good geological websites to explore—museum, college, and geological society sites are usually the most reliable. Check out the websites listed on page 69 of *Eyewitness Rocks & Minerals*.

Museums and societies

Find out what's on at your nearest natural history museum and book a visit. If you can't go there in person, click onto their website and see if they have virtual tours and field trips.

Field trips are just part of most geologists' work. The research starts when they get back to the lab, investigating what they have found.

....

....

....

....

....

....

....

....

....

Scrapbook

Draw pictures of the specimens you find in the field or see in a museum. If you visit a volcano or interesting rock formation, remember to take your camera!

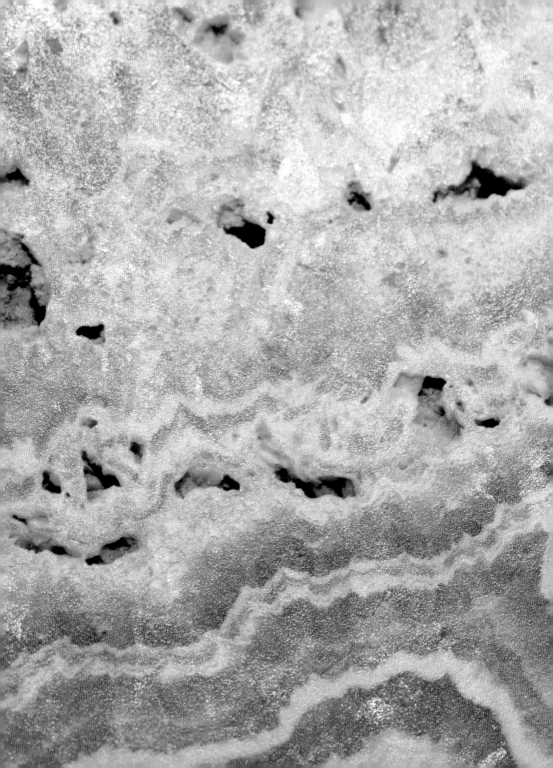

4

PACK MANUAL

Read on and find out how to get the most out
of your interactive expert pack—including
step-by-step instructions for making a set
of your own crystal shapes.

Expert reads

Everything you need to know about getting the most from your interactive expert pack is right here! Written by the experts of today for the experts of tomorrow, these reads will speed you on your journey to discovering the mysteries of Earth and how it works. Read on!

Eyewitness Guide

Your first port of call for all things geological, this museum on a page is where you can be an eyewitness to the incredible wealth of rocks and minerals hidden beneath your feet. Written by experts and illustrated with close-up photographs of collectors' specimens, *Eyewitness Rocks & Minerals* is an essential read for every budding expert.

Wallchart

How are rocks and minerals created? What are their uses in everyday life? Put this chart on your wall at home or at school and the answers to your geological questions will never be far away.

29

Igneous

glass, without crystals

FIELD
Gla
er
s

Rocks on the seashore

AT THE SEASHORE, geological processes can be seen. seashores are backed by cliffs, beneath which is a det that has fallen from above. This is gradually broken up into pebbles, gravel, sand, and mud. Then the various sizes of sediment are deposited separately—this is the raw material for future sedimentary rocks (p. 20).

Pebbles on Chesil Beach, England

SKIMMING STONES
As every kid knows, the best stones for skipping are disk-shaped. They are most likely to be sedimentary or metamorphic rocks, since split easily into sheets.

GRADED GRAINS
On the beach, these pebbles are sorted by wave and tide action. The sand comes from a nearby area. It is pure quartz, the other rock-forming minerals having been washed away by constant wave movement.

Micca schist

Irregularly shaped pyrite nodule

Large coarse pebbles

Slates

LOCAL STONES
These pebbles reflect the local geology, all coming from the rocks of the immediate neighbourhood of the beach where they were colle They are metamorphic rocks that have worn into flat discs.

HIDDEN CRY
Pyrite n
con

Flint daggers
(2,750–1,800 BCE)

Sickle, for reaping crops
(4,000–2,300 BCE)

Flint

Reproduction wooden handle

Cutting edge of flint

FLINT TOOLS
Flint splits in any direction, fractures to a sharp edge, and is fairly widespread. As a result, it was widely adopted by early people to make sharp tools.

Adze, for shaping wood
(10,000–4,000 BCE)

Basaltic lava

Quartz san

Rocks a (broken the Eart wind, to

RO

The rock cycle

New rocks are formed and old rocks are eroded, or worn away, in an endless cycle called the rock cycle, which has been going on for millions of years. Changes to rocks within the Earth are driven by the Earth's internal heat. Changes to rocks on the surface are activated by the weather, driven by energy from the Sun.

Volcanic activity creates new rock

Igneous rocks form

Gabbro

Granite

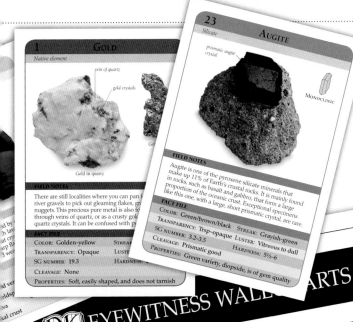

1 GOLD
Native element

vein of quartz

gold crystals

Gold in quartz

FIELD NOTES

There are still localities where you can pan [...] river gravels to pick out gleaming flakes, gr[...] nuggets. This precious pure metal is also fo[...] through veins of quartz, or as a crusty gol[...] quartz crystals. It can be confused with p[...]

FACT FILE

COLOR: Golden-yellow   STREA[...]
TRANSPARENCY: Opaque   LUSTE[...]
SG NUMBER: 19.3   HARDNESS: [...]
CLEAVAGE: None
PROPERTIES: Soft, easily shaped, and does not tarnish

23 AUGITE
Silicate

prismatic augite crystal

MONOCLINIC

FIELD NOTES

Augite is one of the pyroxene silicate minerals that make up 11% of Earth's crustal rocks. It is mainly found in rocks, such as basalt and gabbro, that form a large proportion of the oceanic crust. Exceptional specimens like this one, with a large, short prismatic crystal, are rare.

FACT FILE

COLOR: Green/brown/black
TRANSPARENCY: Trsp–opaque   STREAK: Grayish-green
SG NUMBER: 3.2–3.5   LUSTER: Vitreous to dull
CLEAVAGE: Prismatic good   HARDNESS: 5½–6
PROPERTIES: Green variety, diopside, is of gem quality

Profile Cards
Pull out these handy pocket-size cards and bone up on the essential facts that every expert should know. Use them to test your friends' knowledge, too, or make some of your own cards to add to your collection!

DK EYEWITNESS WALL CHARTS

[ROC]KS & MINERALS

Almost all the rocks on Earth are made up of crystals of naturally occurring chemicals called minerals. Different kinds of rock contain a mixture of different minerals, which give the rock its characteristic color, shape, and properties. Although there are hundreds of types of rock, they all belong to one of three main groups—igneous, sedimentary, or metamorphic—depending on how they were formed.

Layered sandstone

Sandstone

Claystone

Rock particles are deposited in the sea

Sedimentary rocks form

Quartzite

Mica schist

WIND EROSION
Large landforms called "buttes" dot Arizona's Monument Valley. They were formed as winds laden with sediment and rock particles slowly ground away the rock.

CHEMICAL EROSION
Ancient stone buildings, such as the Parthenon in Athens, Greece, often show the effects of drastic weathering. This occurs when chemicals in the air react with, and erode, stone.

ICE EROSION
Glaciers are a major cause of erosion in mountainous regions. Rock fragments frozen in their base scour the underlying rocks as the glacier slowly moves down a valley.

Glassy obsidian, with no or few grains

Holes left by gas bubbles

SHINY OBSIDIAN
Obsidian is a glassy [...] that cools so ra[...] crystals to g[...] characteris[...] was used [...] arrowhea[...]

These [...] of the[...] Irela[...] (eru[...] c[...]

Basaltic ropy lav[...] an extrusive igneous rock

Fine pebbles

Finest pebbles

Quartz sand

Maps and Mapping

New technology is collecting increasingly accurate information about Earth's surface and what lies beneath. Sensors used on land, and carried by planes, satellites, ships, and submersibles, now scan continents, oceans, and the seafloor. This produces data that enables geoscientists to create detailed computer-generated maps. Geologists also work in the field, looking at rocks and using them to interpret structures that lie beneath the surface.

Aerial sensing

Information about Earth's resources is gathered remotely, from airplanes and satellites. This map shows the different minerals in the Animas River Watershed, Colorado, and was created using imaging spectroscopy. A device called a spectroscope is flown over an area to scan and analyze interactions between light and the materials on the ground below. Experts use this information to identify individual minerals.

Exploring under water

The ocean floor features mountains as dramatic as any found on land. This bathymetric map of West Rota submarine volcano, in the Pacific, was produced on a computer, using data gathered by sonar. Research ships survey the ocean floor using instruments that produce multiple beams of sound. The sonar beams bounce back to the ships from seabed surface features, revealing their location, depth, and shape. The map is colored to show the depth from the water surface, from pink at about 1,600 ft (500 m) to dark blue at 1.8 miles (3,000 m).

Your *Eyewitness* map

Modern investigative technology reveals seabed as well as continental geology in your *Eyewitness* map. Techniques ranging from seismology, bathymetry, and imaging spectroscopy to traditional mapping give us this information at a glance. The map's shading shows that ocean floor rocks are no older than 170 million years, while some continental rocks exceed four billion years in age. The color-coded key shows the ages of the world's major rock structures in millions of years, divided into intervals of geological time. Also highlighted are the different types of boundaries along the edges of Earth's tectonic plates, where rocks and minerals have been changed and recycled through time. Look out for the boundaries where most volcanoes are located, the hotspots where volcanic islands have emerged, and the Red Sea Rift, where the African and Arabian plates are pulling apart.

On the ground

Traditional mapping is still part of a geologist's training, and is carried out in the field. Rocks are only visible at outcrops and exposures, but geologists can make calculations about what happens where they disappear below the surface. This is done with the help of a clinometer (shown here), which is used to calculate the angle from the horizontal of folded or faulted strata.

Eyewitness Rocks & minerals Map Rocks & minerals Map Eyewitness

The Changing Earth

THIS GEOLOGICAL MAP reveals the ages of the rocks beneath Earth's continents and oceans, and shows the boundaries of the great tectonic plates that make up the thin upper layer, or crust. The gradual movement of these plates throws up volcanoes, builds mountains, and plunges ocean-floor rocks deep into Earth's interior. Earth's surface is constantly changing.

CONTINENTAL CRUST

The US's Grand Canyon is a window into Earth's past. This vast chasm plunges 7,000 ft (2,134 m) to the Colorado River at its base. Layer upon layer of sedimentary rock strata have been laid down through time, with the youngest at the top and, at the bottom, a deep band of ancient metamorphic "shield" rocks dating back nearly 2 billion years.

OCEANIC CRUST

In the thinner, younger crust below the oceans, powerful forces are at work, in a process called seafloor spreading. Magma wells up along midocean ridges, between the edges of diverging tectonic plates, and hardens to form new rock. The sonar image below shows an underwater mountain chain formed along a ridge. Where tectonic plates collide, oceanic crust is swallowed up, melted, and recycled in the hot mantle below.

Multimedia

Handing in school projects has never been so exciting! Packed with 100 specialized images and facts about rocks and minerals, this clip-art CD will make your homework look so professional you'll be dying to show it off. Go to www.ew.dk.com for more interactive, downloadable information.

Clip-art CD

Olivine

Obsidian

Ruby crystal

DK EYEWITNESS
ROCKS & MINERALS
CLIP ART

EYEWITNESS ROCKS & MINERALS CLIP ART © DORLING KINDERSLEY 2007

For instant pictures open up your clip-art CD, follow the "how to use" instructions, and you'll find the Earth at your fingertips!

Weathering and erosion

Crystal collection

Build on your knowledge of rocks and minerals by assembling these pieces to build six geometric structures of crystals. You'll find step-by-step instructions on the next page.

Before you start assembling the boxes, press out the pieces and fold the card along the score lines. White areas on tabs indicate where pieces should be glued together.

TETRAGONAL
e.g., Diaboleite

MONOCLINIC
e.g., Gypsum

ORTHORHOMBIC
e.g., Olivine

HEXAGONAL / TRIGONAL
e.g., Calcite

TRICLINIC
e.g., Rhodonite

CUBIC
e.g., Pyrite

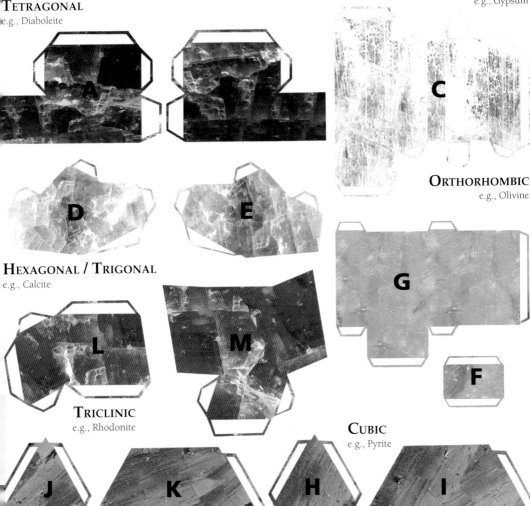

ORTHORHOMBIC

1 Apply glue to tab 1 on piece F and secure to the area on the reverse side of piece G, where indicated.

2 Place the box face down, fold the sides over the middle, and glue tab 2 onto the reverse side, as marked.

3 Open the box and fold tabs 3 and 4 into the middle. Apply glue to tabs 3, 4, and 5, tucking 5 inside the box. Secure the end.

4 Repeat with the opposite end and tabs 6, 7, and 8.

CUBIC

1 Apply glue to tab 1 on section H. Glue onto piece I, as indicated by the white area.

2 Apply glue to tab 2 on section J. Glue onto piece K, as marked.

3 Glue tab 3 on piece H onto the reverse side of piece K, joining all the pieces together.

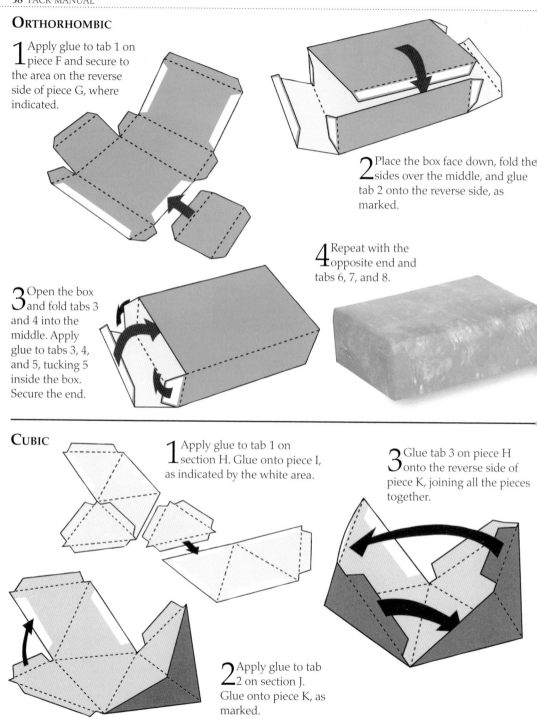

TRICLINIC

1 Apply glue to tab 1 on L, and stick it to the white area on section M.

3 Apply glue to tabs 3, 4, and 5 and press the top down, closing the end of the box.

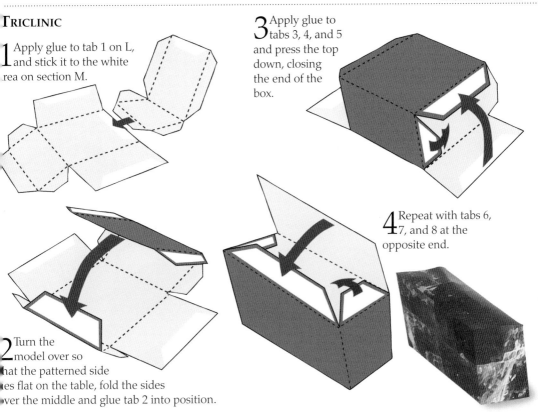

4 Repeat with tabs 6, 7, and 8 at the opposite end.

2 Turn the model over so that the patterned side lies flat on the table, fold the sides over the middle and glue tab 2 into position.

---

5 Repeat step 4 with the bottom half, pieces J and K, gluing tab 5 to secure.

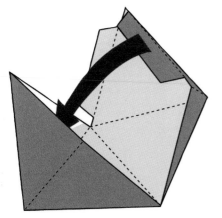

6 Apply glue to tabs 6, 7, and 8, press both pyramid halves together, tucking tabs underneath, and press to secure.

4 Fold the top half, pieces H and I, around, bending them into a pyramid shape. Glue tab 4, as marked.

TETRAGONAL

1 Glue tab 1 on A to the reverse side of piece B, where labeled.

2 Fold the piece over so that the patterned side lies on the table. Fold the sides over the middle and glue tab 2 under piece A, as indicated.

3 Open the box out into a rectangle and apply glue to tabs 3, 4, and 5. Press the square end piece down onto these tabs, as marked, closing the end of the box.

4 Repeat step 3 with the opposite end, gluing tabs 6, 7, and 8 in position.

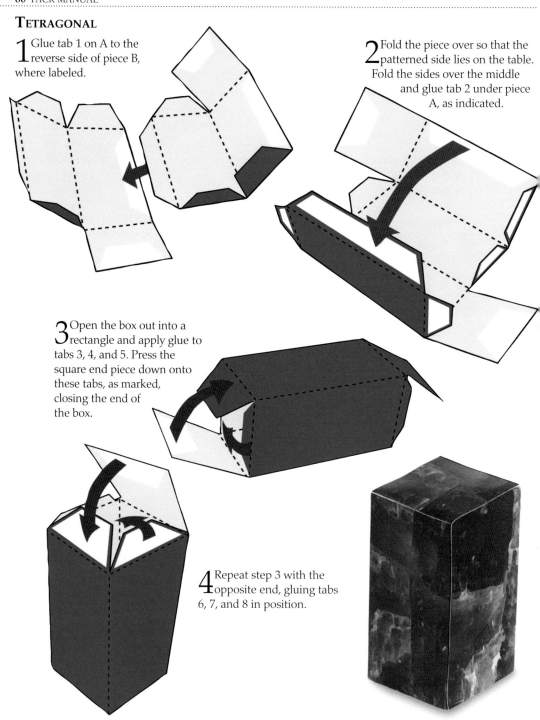

MONOCLINIC

1 Turn piece C over so that the patterned side lies flat on the table. Fold the sides over the middle and glue tab 1 under, as indicated.

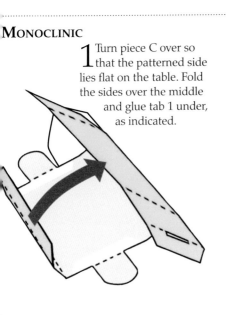

2 Put a spot of glue on tabs 4 and 5 then bend into the middle of the box. Apply glue to tabs 4 and 5, tuck tab 5 into the slot on tab 4, and press down to secure.

3 Repeat step 2 with the other end of the box, folding down tabs 6 and 7 and slotting tab 9 into 8.

HEXAGONAL / TRIGONAL

1 Glue tab 1 on piece E under piece D, as marked.

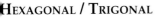

3 Apply glue to the long side— tab 6—and tuck under the edge of piece D, securing in place.

2 Turning the pieces around, glue tabs 2, 4, and 5 onto the areas indicated in white.

4 Apply glue to tabs 7 and 8, fold the flap of the box over the tabs so the fit is good, and press down to secure in position.

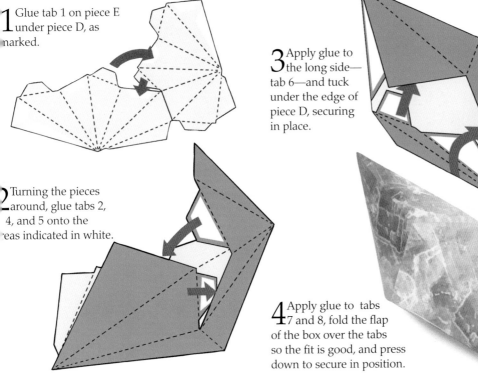

Index

Activity answers

Pages 30–31 Link the rock
1. Taj Mahal, India, Marble.
2. Grand Canyon, US, Red Sandstone.
3. White Cliffs of Dover, England, Flint and chalk.
4. Pyramids at Giza, Egypt, Limestone.
5. Devil's Tower, US, Phonolitic Lava.
6. Giant's Causeway, Northern Ireland, Basaltic Lava. .

Pages 32–33 All that glitters
1. Zircon, F.
2. Ruby, E.
3. Opal, A
4. Diamond, D.
5. Emerald, B.
6. Tourmaline, C.
7. Turquoise, G.

Which cut?
1. Table; 2. Rose; 3. Emerald or step; 4. Pear brilliant; 5. Round brilliant; 6. Cabochon. The two earliest cuts—Table, Cabochon.

Pages 34–35 Tool test
A. Mesolithic adze.
Flint.
Mesolithic period.

Used for shaping wood.
B. Weighted Digging Stick.
Quartzite.
Mesolithic and Neolithic periods.
Used to break up the ground to plant crops or grub up roots.

C. Stone Spindle Whorl.
Stone/Schist
Roman period.
Used to twist thread.

D. Arrowhead.
Flint.
Beaker Period.
Used for hunting.

E. Roman Rotary Quern.
Conglomerate Stone.
Roman period.
Used for grinding corn in the home.

Rock uses
1. Coal, fuel.
2. Slate, building materials, i.e., roofing.
3. Cinnabar or mercury ore, the manufacture of drugs, pigments, insecticides, scientific instruments, as well as in dentistry.
4. Lapis, jewelry.

Pages 36–37 Rock groups
1. Schist, Metamorphic.
2. Granite, Igneous.
3. Sandstone, Sedimentary.
4. Marble, Metamorphic.
5. Obsidian, Igneous.
6. Flint, Sedimentary.
7. Conglomerate, Sedimentary.
8. Gabbro, Igneous.
9. Limestone, Sedimentary.
10. Gneiss, Metamorphic.

Label it
A. Olivine.
B. Wrinkled Lava.
C. Volcanic Bomb.
D. Bedded Tuff.
Olivine is the odd-one-out because it is the only one that is igneous. The others are volcanic.

Pages 38–39 Shape spotters
A. 6; B. 5; C. 4; D. 5; E. 6; F. 1; G. 3; H. 2; I. 3; J. 1; K. 2; L. 4.

Acknowledgments

The publisher would like to thank the following for their kind permission to reproduce their photographs:

(Key: a–above; b–below/bottom; c–center; l–left; r–right; t–top)

Expert Files 1 Dr. Richard Herd. 2–3 **Alamy Images**: Jon Arnold Images. 6–7 **Corbis**: Vittoriano Rastelli. 8 **Corbis**: Kelly-Mooney Photography (bl). **Dr. Richard Herd**: (t). 8–9 **Dr. Richard Herd**. 10 **Dr. Richard Herd** (tl, tr, b). 11 **Dr. Richard Herd** (b). **Montserrat Volcano Observatory**: (t). 12 **Dr. Richard Herd** (tl, tr, b). 13 **Corbis**: Barry Lewis (b). **Dr. Richard Herd**: (t). 14 **Dr. Richard Herd** (l, r). 15 **Dr. Richard Herd**. 16 **Camera Press**: Gamma/Xavier Rossi (t). **PA Photos**: AP/Jamie Plaza (cl). **Science Photo Library**: Eurelios/P. Plailly (b). 17 **Camera Press**: Gamma/Fanny Broadcast (br). **Corbis**: Henry Watkins & Yibran Aragon (bl). **Reuters**: Mario Laporta (t). 18 **Corbis**: Roger Garwood & Trish Ainslie (b). **Getty Images**: Stephen Ferry (c). courtesy of Dr. Sally Gibson, Department of Earth Sciences, **University of Cambridge**: (t). 19 **Corbis**: Bryan Allen (b).

Science Photo Library: British Antarctic Survey (ca); David Vaughan (t). 20 **Science Photo Library**: Mauro Fermariello (bl). 21 **Corbis**: Jonathan Blair (c); Roger Ressmeyer (b). **USGS**: (t). 22 **Corbis**: Bettmann (l); Roger Ressmeyer (tr). **Getty Images**: Time Life Pictures/J. R. Eyerman (br). 23 **Getty Images**: Hulton Archive (l). **Smithsonian Institution**: (r). 24 courtesy of the Archives, **California Institute of Technology**: (t). **Science Photo Library**: (b). 25 **Corbis**: Kipa/Jean Pimentel (t). **Getty Images**: Schostal Archiv/Imagno (b). 26–27 **Corbis**: Guenter Rossenbach. 29 **Camera Press**: Gamma/Fanny Broadcast (t). **PA Photos**: AP/Pier Paolo Cito (b). **Science Photo Library**: Russell D. Curtis (cb). 31 **Corbis**: Bill Ross (bl). 40–41 **DK Images**: courtesy of the Natural History Museum, London. 50–51 **Corbis**: Visuals Unlimited. 54 **NOAA**: (b). **USGS**: (t). 55 **Corbis**: Jonathan Blair (l); P. Wilson (bc).

Map **Corbis**: TWPhoto (br); P. Wilson (cl). **DK Images**:Rowan Greenwood Photography (bc).

PA Photos: AP (clb). Julie Rowland, **University of Auckland**: (crb). **Science Photo Library**: Dr. Ken MacDonald (bl).

Profiles See page 16 of *Rocks & Minerals Profiles*

Wallchart See page 72 of *Eyewitness Rocks & Minerals*

Clip-art CD See the *Credits* file on the CD

All other images © Dorling Kindersley
For further information see:
www.dkimages.com

The publisher would also like to thank:
Ed Merritt for cartography on the Map; **Lynn Bresler** for proofreading & the index; **Neil Lockley & Lisa Stock** for editorial assistance; **Margaret Parrish** for Americanization.